How to Start a Business in

CAMEROON

The Ultimate Guide to Doing Business in Cameroon

Looking to Start a Business in Cameroon?

Known as Africa in Miniature, Cameroon is one of the most beautiful countries of the African continent. Full of resources and diversity, Cameroon remains the largest economy of CEMAC (Economic and Monetary Community of Central Africa). This advantage is also due to its demography (a little more than 20 million inhabitants), area (475 440 km2), geographical situation and diversified economy (agriculture, oil, gas, etc.).

Plenteous are the business prospects available in Cameroon. This youthful country is thick with untapped resources and opportunities. Although not yet a major part of the global economy, this country is growing at a strong pace, and now is a perfect time to enter this market.

The government took on various IMF and World Bank programs, put in place to increase productivity in major sectors of the economy, encourage business investments and ameliorate trade. Although these actions were widely successful, the government is still being urged for more reforms on the economy, and poverty reduction programs.

Cameroon is a country full of possibilities for investment, with a stable currency, a bilingual work force, and a GDP real growth rate of 5.9% as of 2015, as supposed to 5.6% in 2013. Recently, the energy sector in Cameroon opened a natural gas powered electricity generating plant. The government also unlocked substantial resources towards large infrastructure projects such as a deep sea port in Kribi and the Lom Pangar Hydropower Project.

The key contributors to the economy's growth are agriculture, tourism, and the manufacturing sector. Agriculture in Cameroon is one of the biggest employers of the work force. The country is known for its commercial cultivation of crops such as bananas, oil palms, tea, cocoa, sugar crops, coffee and tobacco. Fishing and livestock farming are also major contributors to the economy.

Some of the measures taken by the Cameroonian Government to improve the business climate are:

- The creation of the Ministry of Small and Medium Sized Enterprises, aimed at promoting entrepreneurship;
- The establishment of a "one-stop shop" to simplify bureaucratic requirements for start-ups: CFCE;
- The launch of infrastructural projects to improve roads and energy supply;
- And the ongoing fight against corruption, with the creation of the National Anti-Corruption Commission.

According to reports by the United Nations, Africa is one of the most profitable regions in the World and Cameroon aims to capitalise on this with its various reforms and unlocked resources. Thinking of starting a business in Cameroon, strike while the iron is HOT! Now is the best time.

Looking to Start a Business in Cameroon? iii

CHAPTER 1: CAMEROON 1

General Presentation 1

Brief History 2

Cameroon's Geography 2

Cameroon's Culture 3

Cameroon's Economic Climate 3

Africa in Miniature 4

Threats to Cameroon 4

Cameroon and the World 4

CHAPTER 2: THRIVING SECTORS FOR INVESTMENTS AND BUSINESS 6

Investment Climate 6

Foreign Financing 6

Untapped Resources and Resource Destruction 6

Oil Industry 7

Energy Sector 7

Tourism Industry 8

Financial Sector 9

Agribusiness 10

Education Sector 11

Mining Industry 11

The Infrastructure Sector 12

E-Commerce 12

CHAPTER 3: FRANCHISING AND START-UPS 13

Franchising in Cameroon 13

Startups in Cameroon 13

Startup business Ideas 15

CHAPTER 4: TOURISM 17

Central Region 18

Touristic Attractions : 18

Littoral Region 19

East Region: 20

Ecotourism: 20

North region: 21

Others : 21

West region 22

Adamaoua Region 24

Falls and lakes 24

Mountains, caves and rocks: 25

The festivals : 25

South region 25

North-west region 26

Tourist attractions : 27

South-West Region 27

Ecotourism: 27

Seaside tourism:..28

Cultural Tourism:..28

Sports Tourism: 29

Other Sites:..29

Touristic sites: 29

Infrastructure 31

Corruption 31

Ease of Doing Business..31

CHAPTER 6: STEP-BY-STEP BUSINESS REGISTRATION PROCESS 32

Theoretical creation 32

GOOD TO KNOW:..34

Practical creation 35

CHAPTER 7: LAWS AND REGULATORY BODIES 39

Laws and Regulations 39

Newspapers Legislation 39

OHADA 39

Free economic zones..39

Regulatory Bodies 39

CHAPTER 8: TIPS AND ADVICE 40

Resources for Further Research..43

THINGS TO DO WITH DOCUMENT:.............................Error! Bookmark not defined.

CHAPTER 1: CAMEROON

General Presentation

Cameroon is located in Central Africa, north of the Gulf of Guinea. The country is bordered to the west by Nigeria, to the south by Congo (Brazzaville), Gabon and Equatorial Guinea, to the east by the Central African Republic, to the north-east by Chad, and to the north by Lake Chad.

Cameroon's southern and coastal areas are characterized by dense vegetation, a vast river system, and a hot, humid climate with abundant rainfall.

In 2015, the number of births in Cameroon exceeded the number of deaths by about 591,000, creating a natural population increase. However, due to external migration, the population declined by almost 13,000. In 2016, the population growth was estimated at 2.58%, with a large portion under the age of 25.

Official Name: Republic of Cameroon

Current President: Paul Biya

Total Geographical Area: 475,440 kilometers

Population Density: 49.7/km2

Capital Cities:

Yaoundé – Political capital

Douala – Economic capital

Official Languages: With over 250 dialects, the official languages are French and English

Currency: FCFA – Franc de la Communauté Financière Africaine

Time zone: WAT (UTC+1)

Calling Code: +237

Population: About 24 million

Brief History

The legacy of Cameroon's ethnic diversity can be traced back to 8,000 BCE with the migration of the Baka people into modern-day Cameroon's borders. So its earliest inhabitants were the Baka, also known as the Pygmies.

In the 15th century, Portuguese explorers named the shrimp-laden area near the mouth of the Wouri River, the Rio dos Camaroes ("River of Prawns"). Over time, this was shortened in English to Cameroon.

By 1884, Cameroon became Germany's colony and was named Kamerun, with its first capital in Buea. After World War I, a League of Nations mandate partitioned the colony of Kamerun into two sections. France gained the larger geographical share, and Britain a land bordering Nigeria. Cameroon gained its independence in 1960, with Ahmadou Ahidjo as its first president. Paul Biya became Cameroon's second president in 1982.

Cameroon's Geography

The country of Cameroon is divided into five major geographic zones: coast, rainforest, mountain, desert, and savanna. These zones are distinguished by dominant physical, climatic, and vegetative features.

Coast: The coastal plain extends 15 to 150 kilometers inland from the Gulf of Guinea, and has an average elevation of 90 meters (295 ft.). Exceedingly hot and humid with a short dry season, this belt is densely forested and includes some of the wettest places on earth.

Rainforest: The South Cameroon Plateau rises from the coastal plain, to an average elevation of 650 meters. Equatorial rainforest dominates this region. This area is part of the Atlantic Equatorial coastal forests ecoregion.

Mountains: Cameroon has an irregular chain of mountains, hills, and plateaus known as the Cameroon range. This extends from Mount Cameroon on the coast (highest point at 4,095 meters) to Lake Chad on Cameroon's northern border. This region has a mild climate, with high rainfall. The soil here could be Cameroon's most fertile, particularly around Mount Cameroon, which is volcanic. The area of the Lake Nyos, which belched carbon dioxide and killed thousands of people, has been delineated: Cameroon's Highlands forests ecoregion by the World Wildlife Fund.

Savanna: Its distinctive vegetation is savanna scrub grass. An arid region with sparse rainfall and high median temperatures, its average elevation in the southern plateau is 1,100 meters (3,609 ft.), and its average temperature ranges from 22 °C to 25 °C, with high rainfall between April and October. The northern lowland region extends from the edge of the Adamawa to Lake Chad, with an average elevation of 300 to 350 meters (984 to 1,148 ft.).

Cameroon's Culture

Population: Cameroon has about 250 ethnic groups and languages. The Baka, also known as the Pygmies, are the longest continuous indigenous people, next to the Cameroon Highlanders, the Equatorial Bantus, the Kirdis and Fulanis, the Northwestern Bantus and the Eastern Nigritic. Other Africans contribute up to 13% of the population. Life expectancy here is about 56 years, with 50.1% of the population being female and 49.9% male.

Religion: Cameroon's population is mostly separated into two major religious groups: Christians and Muslims. Up to 70% identify as Christian (Catholic, Protestant and other Christian groups). Christian believers are mainly in the southern and western regions. Most of the 21% of Cameroon's population who are of the Islamic faith live in the north of Cameroon. About 6% of Cameroonians still maintain indigenous belief systems. The smallest percentage is non-believers, at about 3%.

Football and Music: Cameroon is well known for its professional football teams and players. The country has qualified 7 times for the World Cup, making it up to the quarter-finals in 1990. It has appeared 17 times at the African Cup of Nations and went ahead to win in 1984, 1988, 2000, 2002, and 2017. Some of its most popular players are Samuel Eto'o, Roger Milla, Patrick Mboma, Thomas Nkono, Rigobert Song, Alex Song, and many more. The female football team is also coming up brilliantly.

Cameroon's music is also very popular. Its most famous rhythms are Makossa, Bikutsi, Benskin, and new music styles created by the younger generation. Some of its internationally acclaimed artists are Manu Dibango, Richard Bona, Petit Pays, and many more.

Cameroon's Economic Climate

The country's economy is greatly regulated and dependent on the export of commodities. With the expansion of oil, timber, and coffee exports, Cameroon's economy has continued to improve. However, corruption and environmental degradation remain a concern.

In June of 2000, the World Bank provided about $200 million to build a $3.7 billion pipeline connecting the oil fields in neighboring Chad, with Cameroon's coast.

Also, in 2006, Nigeria finally turned over the disputed oil-rich Bakassi peninsula to Cameroon, after the International Court of Justice ruled in Cameroon's favor.

With its modest oil resources and advantageous agricultural conditions, Cameroon is one of the best-endowed primary commodity economies in Sub-Saharan Africa. And despite falling global oil prices, oil still accounts for about 40% of export earnings.

Cameroon's highlands region is rich in volcanic soils, which is a major advantage for the cultivation of crops.

Africa in Miniature

Cameroon is known as "Africa in Miniature" due to its geological and cultural diversity. It hosts all the major climates and vegetation of the African continent: desert, rainforest, coast, savanna, and mountain. Nearly 90% of the African ecosystems can be found in Cameroon.

Besides its 250 languages, cultures and traditions, Cameroon's official languages are two of the world's most popular languages: English and French.

Threats to Cameroon

For some time, Boko Haram was considered a serious threat to the country's stability, as they had conducted attacks in Cameroon's Far North Region, where the country shares a border with Nigeria. This group is an Islamist sect based in Nigeria, which is opposed to Western education, political philosophy, and society.

Also recently, an uprising of Cameroon's English-speaking regions took place. For some time, the population of the south-west and north-west regions, which represents about one fifth of Cameroon's population, had been denouncing marginalization and even discrimination towards them, by the government. However, this all took a more serious turn in 2017, as massive protests across these regions started taking place. The activists are calling for secession and the creation of a new country, which they have named Ambazonia.

Cameroon and the World

Bakassi is a peninsula on the Gulf of Guinea, which for a long time was the cause of much strife between Cameroon and neighboring Nigeria. In 1981, Cameroon and Nigeria nearly went to war due to a

4

dispute over who owned the peninsula. To find a resolution, the matter was introduced to the International Court of Justice in 1994.

In 2002, the ICJ ruled on the boundary, siding with Cameroon. In 2006, President Paul Biya and President Olusegun Obasanjo of Nigeria resolved the dispute in talks with UN Secretary General at the time, Kofi Annan.

Cameroon is a member of the African Union; the Commonwealth; the African, Caribbean and Pacific Group of States; the Non-Aligned Movement; Organisation Internationale de la Francophonie; the Organisation of Islamic Cooperation; the United Nations, and the World Trade Organization.

CHAPTER 2: THRIVING SECTORS FOR INVESTMENTS AND BUSINESS

Investment Climate

With the economic climate opening up and thriving, now is a great time to invest in this youthful nation. Going from a country with a business environment dominated by Europe for so many years, we can observe today the emergence of new investors such as China, Morocco, Nigeria, Tunisia, Algeria, South Africa, and many more.

One sector that is in real need of investment is the Sector of Infrastructure, which, once improved, will play a significant role in the development of other sectors. There are also specific opportunities in tourism, finance, agriculture, education, and mining.

Foreign Financing

With its new investment code enacted in April 2013, the government introduced new tax incentives, cancelled the minimum investment capital requirement, and enhanced export incentives and value-add opportunities.

Investing in the banking sector is one of the easiest ways to access the country's emerging economy. Private investments could help reduce pressures on the overall economy, which would, in turn, encourage growth. However, this cannot be considered a substitution for larger private capital participation. Financing companies are what Cameroon needs the most to boost its economy, and this can be achieved through direct participation and expertise.

Untapped Resources and Resource Destruction

Cameroon is a resource-rich country with vast agricultural potentials. There are 22 million hectares of forests, about 70 species of wood, and large quantities of water available.

The country has untapped mining resources of bauxite, natural gas, rutile, iron, zinc oxide gold, diamonds, and cobalt. Also, it is heavily dependent on revenues generated from oil, timber, and agricultural products, and could do more in the future with smart investments by entrepreneurs.

Poaching has been identified as a major problem in Cameroon, due to inadequate security.

Also, each year, fires and commercial exploitation of the forests result in the elimination of about 200,000 hectares. Even within reserved lands, the forest experiences destruction.

In the semiarid northern rangelands, overgrazing is degrading the overall quality of the ground vegetation. However, while these may seem like a barrier to many, these problems actually represent business opportunities.

Oil Industry

Following the settlement of the border dispute with Nigeria over the Bakassi Peninsula, Cameroon is now located in a prime area for transit within the Central African Region and West Africa. The Chad-Cameroon Oil Pipeline transports Doba Crude oil from Doba in Tchad, to an export facility in Kribi Cameroon.

The SONARA (Société Nationale de Raffinage) in Limbe, is Cameroon's sole refinery and refines only about 21% of the country's crude oil.

The SNH (Société Nationale des Hydrocarbures) is the regulatory body for oil and gas.

From a low point of 75,000 barrels per day in 2008, oil production in Cameroon has rebounded to about 100,000 barrels per day in 2016. Cameroon's finance ministry reveals that during the 2017 fiscal year, the oil revenues it generated were FCFA385.9 billion.

Also, when it comes to non-oil revenues, the general performance is respectable. It was reported that by the end of the year 2017, non-oil revenues were FCFA2,671.2 billion, in comparison to FCFA2,413.3 billion the previous year. This represents a 99.4% success rate, as the target for non-oil revenues was FCFA2,688.2 billion. There are major opportunities for investors in infrastructure development projects.

Ministry: Ministry of Mines and Technological Development https://minmidt-gov.net/en/index.html

Energy Sector

Cameroon has a great goal, which is to become an emerging market economy by 2035. However, a huge amount of effort will be required in order for this to become a reality, starting with reforming Cameroon's struggling energy sector.

Following pressures from the International Monetary Fund, the government reduced fuel subsidies. Indeed, fuel subsidies had grown tremendously in three years, and all economic indicators had been pointing to the unsustainability of the policy in place at the time.

A proposal for a liquefied natural gas plant has created a lot of buzz in the country. With the country refining only about 21% of its crude oil, the capacity of the refinery is being increased, so that greater results are expected once the current projects are completed.

Ministry: Ministry of Water Resources and Energy

Tourism Industry

Known as Africa in Miniature, Cameroon is an explosion of colors, diversity, and beauty. With Cameroon's cultural heritage and the diversity of its landscape, the country is a real touristic destination. In addition, Cameroon's population is young, dynamic, friendly, fun, and multilingual.

Tourism in general contributes significantly to the world's economy and employment. The World Travel & Tourism Council's 2017 research reports that tourism contributes to the GDP even more than the automotive industry across the globe – three times as much in America and two times as much in Europe.

In Cameroon, tourism is one of the major contributors to the national economy. Statistics from 2015 and 2016 reveal that tourism contributed 3.1 percent in 2015 and 5.3 percent in 2016 towards the national Public Investment Budget (PIB), and contributed 7 percent towards employment in 2015.

Despite the recent crisis in the English-speaking regions and issues in the Far North at the frontier with Nigeria, Cameroon is still said to be a peaceful country and a wonderful touristic destination.

However, the industry's contribution, which is growing steadily, is still relatively insignificant, in comparison to the country's potential. Its main challenge is believed to be the country's lack of exposure. Not many people know much about Cameroon, its resources, people, and potential.

This industry is full of investment opportunities, and here are a few ideas:

- Infrastructure and road improvement/maintenance

- Real estate: hotels, furnished apartments, camps

- Online and physical tourism agencies

- Transport: taxi services, public transport services, car rental companies, boats and canoe rental services, helicopter transportation services

- Souvenir shops

- Language translation services

- Cultural holiday activities in different regions

- Travel guides

- Security/bodyguard agencies

- Excursion agencies

- Language or dialect lessons/schools

- Traditional dance lessons/schools

It is apt to say that with a bit more publicity, exposure, and investments, the industry has the potential to become a major player in the overall country's economy, not to mention the advantages for the local people. For example:

- Maintenance of the touristic sites

- Jobs for the locals

- Improvement and maintenance of infrastructure (roads)

Ministry: Ministry of Tourism www.mintour.gov.cm

Financial Sector

Cameroon's growing financial sector is the largest in the CEMAC (Central African Economic and Monetary Community) region. However, Cameroon's financial system is still quite underdeveloped. Despite its numerous banks, insurance companies, micro-financial institutions, and a promising stock exchange, Cameroon is still somewhat disconnected from the international financial system.

The banking sector is highly concentrated and dominated by foreign banks. These banks achieve 20% or more on returns, whilst local banks struggle to break even. It is believed that this is due to a lack of management expertise, lack of capital, and faulty risk management. The banks therefore have difficulties investing in small companies and ultimately doing business with citizens in general.

The population points to access to cash as a major impediment to business, since interest loans are hard to get. Banks on the other hand attribute this to the lack of quality bankable projects and companies, as well as non-performance on loans in past transactions, which had caused them to further reduce access to credit.

The majority of financial transactions in Cameroon are done in cash. However, a fast-growing number of people own a bank account.

Ministry: Ministry of finance www.minfi.gov.cm

Agribusiness

Opportunities in agribusiness abound, as Cameroon is the agricultural hub of the CEMAC region, with about 37 million citizens living in the six member states (Congo Brazzaville, Chad, Central African Republic, Equatorial Guinea, Gabon, and Cameroon). This is without mentioning neighboring Nigeria and its 194 million habitants.

With a mass of arable land that's over 65% of the land and two-thirds rainfall a year, Cameroon is the perfect place to invest in agribusiness. Investments made in processing and technological upgrades could push the country into the upper ranks of agribusiness in Africa.

Some of Cameroon's agricultural bounties are cash crops. Not only is this nation the fifth in the world for cocoa growth, it also boasts plentiful cotton, bananas, peanuts, coffee, beans, rubber, and different types of grains, plants, vegetables, and tubers.

Palm oil and oilseed processing can be used to make oil-based products and can be useful for feed manufacturing. With investments in processing equipment, packaging, and improved branding of products like cocoa and coffee, the agribusiness sector in Cameroon could be a lot more lucrative.

In addition to cash crops, Cameroon has livestock and timber. The country has an array of livestock farms, including mixed cattle, sheep, goats, horses, donkeys, pigs, and poultry.

Timber export has grown since the early 1990s, but the amount of illegal exporting, as well as deforestation of the rain forests, is a challenge. Funding is needed to build the strength of the Forest Crimes Monitoring Unit and help Cameroon's loggers create sustainable practices.

Ministry: Ministry of Commerce and Industry

Education Sector

About 75% of the population above the age of 15 can read and write. Here, education is provided by public and private institutions. The Ministries of Basic Education, Secondary Education, Employment and Vocational Training and the Ministry of Higher Education are the institutions in charge of education in Cameroon. The private sector includes religious and private lay institutions.

Investment in education, just as in any country, is key to bringing more success to the greater population, building the economy, and creating solid global relationships. Opportunities for foreign investors in private education are immense and encouraged by the government.

Ministry: www.minesec.cm, www.minedub.cm

Mining Industry

The Cameroonian soil is rich with a diversity of mineral resources. Its main mineral resources or commodities are aluminum, cobalt, bauxite, limestone, diamond, gold, iron ores, nickel, uranium, petroleum, and pozzolana,

The mining industry is regulated by the Ministry of Mines, Industry and Technological Development. Thus, for information on licenses, taxes, mining and petroleum codes, it would be best to contact the Ministry directly.

The Mining Taxation Scheme is regulated by three laws:

- The law 001 of the 16th April 2001 on the Mining Code

- The decree 2002/048/PM of the 26th March 2002, fixing the modalities for application of the Mining Code

- The general Code of Taxes, as well as its diverse modifications

Even though abused by traffickers, and despite the government granting about 150 exploitation licenses, Cameroon's mining potential remains largely untapped. According to numerous entrepreneurs, a lot needs to be done in the infrastructural sector.

Revenues from the extractive industries accounted for 5.43% of the GDP and 33.23% of total exports in 2015. EITI's report discloses that there are 25 companies active in the oil, gas, and mining industries.

Production-sharing contracts are awarded by the SNH, on the basis of competitive tender or direct negotiations. Mining licenses are awarded on a "first come first served" basis. 54 new research permits and 36 quarrying permits were awarded in 2015. In February 2017, Cameroon launched its online mining cadaster.

Ministry: Ministry of Mine, Industry and Technological Development www.minmidt-gov.net

The Infrastructure Sector

Upgrading transport, roads, and ports is high on the government's agenda. A high budget has been allocated to infrastructure, particularly the construction of the Yaoundé-Douala Highway, the Bamenda Ring Road, and the Menchum Dam. These are just some of the government's major projects. A lot therefore still needs to be done in this sector, as mentioned whilst discussing the previous industries. This represents major opportunities for private investors.

E-Commerce

As of March 2017, 4,909,178 of the population had an internet connection in Cameroon, according to IWS. This represents 20% of the population in the year 2017, up from 18% the previous year, and 15.9% in 2015. The number of homes with smartphones has increased to 72.2%, just in the second half of 2016, giving Cameroon one of the highest rates of smartphone use in Africa.

And yet, there is a real need in the e-commerce sector. Indeed, although improvement was observed in 2016, thanks to companies such as Sellam Quick who are trying to bring a solution to this problem, access to goods and services online remains a problem for Cameroonians. E-commerce is virtually non-existent in the country (online shopping, etc.), whilst the populations' desire for online products and services keeps growing.

CHAPTER 3: FRANCHISING AND START-UPS

Besides the thriving sectors for investment and business opportunities discussed in Chapter Two, there are many more openings and opportunities that welcome entrepreneurs or simply business-minded people.

In a bid to encourage entrepreneurs and new businesses, Cameroon's government has put in place incentives such as tax exoneration, a free-trade zone, the free transfer of proceeds, national investment support schemes and custom excise benefits. The government has also given the freedom to both local and foreign companies to secure their brands with the OAPI (African Intellectual Property Organization), as well as commercial names, from any infringement by third parties.

Franchising in Cameroon

Franchising here is still pretty much an unknown territory, which has yet to be explored, both by local and foreign companies. Cameroonians still struggle with the concept of franchising, as it is still in its early stages.

Startups in Cameroon

Cameroon is a continuously growing market, full of diversity and opportunities. Its people are very open and welcoming to new and innovative ideas. Therefore, even a startup with a novelty product or service has the same chance to grow and be successful as any mainstream or conventional business. All that's essential, besides the usual requirements, is a bit of boldness, a good understanding of the people (so as to know how best to bring the product forward), and a decent understanding of the country and its multiple cultures.

So, how does one go about establishing a new business? Here are a few tips:

Your Business Idea: Your first step would have to be the business idea. Figure out what you want to do, what needs to be done to accomplish it, and if you have the capacity to put in the work it requires. The business could be a service or product that solves a problem experienced by the community or an innovative product or service that will need to be introduced to the public.

Your Business Plan: Developing a strong business plan and considering all aspects of the proposed business cannot be overemphasized, when planning to start a business in Cameroon. With a well-thought-out business plan, the goals and objectives are clearly stated and can serve as reference points.

Here are a few benefits of a business plan:

- Strategy reminder: Your business plan will summarize the main points of your strategy.

- Clear business objectives: You can use your plan to define and manage specific objectives.

- Clarity on interdependencies: Keep track of what needs to be done and in what order.

- Tracking through milestones: Keep track of dates and deadlines.

- Delegating: The business plan will clarify who should be responsible for what.

Your Team: Creating a startup is a massive job that will require you to juggle quite a few roles. That being said, not many people have the skills et for every role. Besides, trying to take on too many roles could be detrimental to your company. So as much as you might have to take on a few responsibilities, especially at the start of your business, building a team and the right team must be part of your immediate plans. So, once you've had an honest conversation about what skills you lack, find people who believe in your idea and have the skills you require. You could do this by putting up ads online, or on your social media pages, or by simply asking friends and family.

Your Business Location: The location you choose for your business should be easily reached and accessible to your target market, ideally, even if yours is an online business.

Your Capital: The first four steps are crucial, for anyone planning to build a successful business. But when it comes to the capital, it all depends on the type of business that is being set up. Some online or service-oriented businesses might not necessarily require "capital" in the early stages or to start off. However, for most businesses, finances would be essential to start and run the business (purchasing or producing goods, as well as maintaining operations).

There are different ways one could raise capital for a startup:

- Get or stay in a job and save up, whilst planning and working on the business

- Look for an angel investor who would believe in the idea and fund it

- Start a little side business from which you can save up

- Ask family and friends for little amounts, which could ultimately amount to the required capital

- Or simply partner with someone who will put in the funds

It is not advisable to start a business with a loan.

Your Business Registration: The business will have to be registered with the local authorities (See Chapter 6).

Your Business Bank Account: This account will be used for business transactions such as paying bills, receiving monies from customers in exchange for goods or services, and paying employees.

Startup business Ideas

As discussed earlier, Cameroon is an emerging country, full of opportunities, with a people open to change and innovation. Therefore, the few ideas listed below are in no way a representation of the extent of opportunities available:

- Transport business: Private taxi/cab offices, cars/boats/helicopter rental agencies

- Licensed football agency: Sports and football in particular are an important part of the Cameroonian culture. However, there is a need for licensed agencies.

- Catering services: Tea parties, cocktail parties, buffets, etc

- Real estate: Besides being a sure investment, acquiring a piece of land in Cameroon is relatively affordable, depending on the region. For example, there are no shopping malls in the country. Also, there is a great demand for affordable furnished apartments.

- Branding company

- PR and marketing business

- Original fashion design brand

- Branded natural products for skin and hair care

- Spa treatment facility/service

- E-commerce: Facilitating access to goods and services from around the world to Cameroonians and vice versa

- Procurement and logistics

- Tourism and travel agencies (physical or online)

- Events planning

- Interior designing

CHAPTER 4: TOURISM

In a continent of 54 countries, Cameroon, with a population of about 24.5 million, has the second largest number of tribes and languages (dialects), after Nigeria which is the largest country in Africa with a population of 194.5 million.

Cameroon has about 250 languages and tribes. With each tribe, comes very distinct traditions, cultures, cuisines, and ways of doing things.

Cameroonians in general are a very happy people, welcoming, creative, curious, and adventurous.

Besides its amazing sceneries, touristic sites, cultural diversity and folkloric population, one important aspect that is sure to stick with you after visiting Cameroon would have to be its variety of meals.

Cameroon offers some of the best (if not the best), diverse and creative cuisine in Africa. Some of these meals are better cooked on firewood or banana leaves (koki, mais de pistache) and others best enjoyed on the side of the road (suya, poisson braise, beignets/haricot). This is to say that food is very important in Cameroon.

Some of the most famous Cameroonian dishes are ndole, poulet DG, eru, sanga, okok, poisson braise, peanut stew, mbongo chobi, mais de pistache, koki, ekwang, egusi soup, achu, puff puff, and beans.

There is also a very good variety of national and foreign restaurants, such as Nigerian, Senegalese, Italian, Chinese, French, Lebanese, etc.

Tourists have a choice of residing either in a hotel or in a furnished apartment during their stay. For transportation around the city, there are car hire companies (with the option of a driver), as well as public and private taxi services.

Cameroon also has different ways of traveling around the country: by air (there are five functional airports, amongst which two international airports: Yaoundé Nsimalen and Douala International Airport), by train, by road, by sea (Cameroon has ports in Douala, Garoua, Limbe, and Kribi).

Different types of tourism are possible in Cameroon: seaside tourism or seaside resorts, agricultural tourism, safari, cultural tourism, and many more.

Activities you can enjoy in Cameroon:

- Sightseeing around the different regions

- Attending cultural or traditional events

- Enjoying the beach: Cameroon has two main seaside cities, Limbe and Kribi

- Visiting the pygmies in the Eastern Forests

- Enjoying the liveliness, fun, and ambience of the big cities: Yaoundé and Douala

- Safari in the Far North Region

Cameroon is divided into 10 regions: Central, Littoral, East, North, West, South, Adamawa, South-West, North-West, Far North. Each of these regions has its touristic sites and main city. Here are just a few of Cameroon's tourist attractions:

Central Region

Yaoundé, county town of the region, is also the capital of the country and home to all institutions.

The Central Region is notable for its humid climate, lush vegetation and multiple traditions of its people. This region is ideal for excursions, ecotourism, and agro-tourism.

County-town: Yaoundé

The central region is notable for its humid climate, lush vegetation and multiple traditions of its people. This region is ideal for excursions, ecotourism and agro tourism.

Touristic Attractions :

- The Lorraine Cross or Leclerc Monument, which symbolizes the call to the gathering of the Gaullists

- The National Museum, or old Presidential Palace

- The building of ALCAMOR in which the autonomy of East Cameroon was celebrated in May 1957

- The statue of Charles Atangana, last great chief of the Ewondo and Bene tribes

- The Reunification Monument, built in 1972, in memory of the 1961 reunification of both parts of Cameroon: Anglophone and Francophone

- The Ebogo site is a bank of the Nyong River, designed for water sports and canoe trips. On the road, there are workshops of basketry and traditional musical instruments

- The Mefou Park: Here are found dozens of monkey species

- The Nachtigal Falls, Ndokom, Ninoum, Mbam, Mpoume, and Mbila

- The Sanaga Cascades

- Mangrove Bay of Mbega

- So'o Bridge

Akok Bekoe, a rock made up of a multitude of very spectacular caves, located in Bikoe Village

Littoral Region

Douala, county town of the region, is Cameroon's liveliest city and the country's commercial capital. Full of life, events, and business opportunities, this city is home to Cameroon's main sea port and international airport.

County town : Douala

About a third of Cameroon's economic activities occur in this region. Its main cities are Nkongsamba, Edéa, Yabassi, and Douala, Douala being the country's largest city.

Douala, which thrives in businesses and industries, used to be a small fishing community that the Portuguese, (the first Europeans to set foot in Cameroon) encountered in the 15th century. This started a long tradition of trading between coastal rulers and Europeans.

Now Cameroon's principal port, Douala handles almost all of the country's maritime traffic, and is the main point of entry for import and export in Cameroon. It also hosts one of Cameroon's main international airports, Douala International Airport (the other being Yaoundé Nsimalen).

Douala, with its pulsating atmosphere and its pleasant tropical ambience, is great for nightlife, as it is packed with lively bars, clubs, cabarets, and restaurants.

At the center of the city is Akwa, the principal commercial district. Central Douala is divided into district neighborhoods, mainly named after the original ruling families. These include the upmarket residential quarter Bonapriso, administrative sector Bonanjo, and industrial Bonaberi.

The highlight of the year for the Sawa people and a real tourist attraction, is the Ngondo, a traditional festival and ritual of the coastal people. The festival brings the Sawa people of the Littoral region together, during the first week of December. It's a huge and absolutely spectacular traditional party, which has been in existence since 1830.

East Region:

Called the Region of the Rising Sun, this region is dominated by tall trees, with nearly 1,500 plant species, as well as more than 500 animal species. It has also been declared a World Heritage of Humanity. The Eastern Region is populated, among other tribes, by the Pygmies, the first inhabitants of the region, who engage in gathering and hunting. A friendly and welcoming people living in the forest, the pygmies have kept their ancient way of life.

County town: Bertoua

Ecotourism:

- Dja Resort: Surrounded by the river Dja, great biodiversity and variety of primates.

- Lobeke National Park: Kingdom of several types of birds, gorillas and other mammals.

- The Boumba Beck, Mbam Djerem and Nki resorts.

- The undergrowth of Madouma.

Tourism of adventure : Safari photos (Unique images are offered to visitors in the savannahs).

Waterfalls, cascades and lakes: Boden waterfalls, Ndong waterfalls, Batouri lake (Sport fishing and canoe trips), Mokounounou lake, Boumba waterfall, Mali Fall, Sanaga banks, the falls of Nki.

Mountains, caves and peaks: The Pandi Mountains (rich in fauna, have been identified as male and female.), The Marian sanctuary (arranged by Catholic missionaries.), The caves of Mbartoua, Mvanda, Esseng and Timbe.

Others: The hippopotamus pond of Ndélélé, The artisanal gold mines, The steps of Nika, The camp of the Pygmies of Mayo, The city of Lomié with its colonial architecture.

North region:

This region has a typically Sudanese climate. With its three national parks, Benoue, Bouba Ndjida, and Faro, the region of North Cameroon has the most representative specimens of the African fauna.

County town: Garoua

Cynegetic tourism: Sport hunting and sport fishing can be practiced in the 28 specially developed areas around national parks.

- The National Park of Bouba Ndjida: It shelters most species peculiar to this region of Central Africa: derby elans, elephants, giraffes, lions, panthers, buffaloes, topis, hyenas, baboons, vervets, patas, and many more

- The Bénoué National Park has four camps: Black Buffalo, Bel Elan, Grand Captain and Kobas

- The National Park of Faro: You can find the same animal species as in the parks of Bouba Ndjida and Bénoué, but also a diverse birdlife including turtledoves, guinea fowl, blackbirds, rock chickens and gangas

Cultural tourism: The cultural diversity of the northern population can be seen in their cuisine, their very authentic habitats, their dress style, and the many traditional chiefdoms.

- The Lamidat of Rey Bouba is part of the UNESCO World Heritage.

- The Lamidats of Garoua and Demsa are also famous for their cultural riches.

- The Gouma dance: This topless dance has an international reputation.

- The Guider people, renowned for their pottery, are also known for their traditional dances after the harvest.

Others :

- The Laggdo Dam and the wonderful Damans Island.

21

- Kala Kafinarou Lake, whic is a depression formed by Mayo Louti and Mayo Kebbi

- Mount Tinguelin, very picturesque mountain dominating the city of Garoua.

- The population of Toro village in the laminat of Demsa, which remains refractory to any modern penetration.

- The artisanal center of Garoua, which is well furnished with art.

West region

The Western Region is the cradle of the Bamileke and Bamoun ethnic groups. Wonderfully endowed by nature, it is a hilly region crossed by beautiful rivers, interspersed with falls. It also presents a series of rounded mountains, legacies of ancient volcanoes. The climate here is temperate.

A region of tradition and culture, west Cameroon is characterized by a wealth of craftsmanship: pipes, terracotta utensils, figurines and copper masks, stools decorated with pearls, and picturesque costumes. Foumban is the headquarters of Cameroonian crafts.

County town : Bafoussam

Cultural tourism: Museums and traditional chiefdoms are the main attractions of the region, which is very representative of the importance of ancestral culture still respected.

- Sultanate of Foumban: Commonly called the "City of Arts," Foumban is the capital of the Bamoun Kingdom. Its royal palace, a beautiful mix of architectural styles, is a must-see attraction. Built in 1917, the king of the Bamouns still lives there today. The famous Foumban museum tells the story of one of the oldest Black African kingdoms and its population of warriors. This story is told through more than 3,000 art representations and historical pieces of Bamoun culture.

- Chiefdom of Bandjoun: The architecture of this chieftaincy is certainly the most monumental and the most majestic of the Bamileke country. The central building is a set surmounted by a heavy conical roof, with furniture mostly made of bamboo. There is also a rich museum.

- Chiefdom of Bafoussam: This chieftaincy was created around 1200 by the peoples originating from the Tikar plain. It has a rich collection of cultural, religious, political, and social objects that serve to express the power of the current ruler.

- Bamendjou chiefdom: It consists of crossed bamboo huts, a large Nemmoh hut decorated with carved wooden elements, and a colonial style palace built at the beginning of the 20th century.

Festivals: The predominance of traditional festivals and ceremonies allows the local culture to be experienced through masks, costumes, dances, and traditional rites. The population lives at the rhythm of cultural and traditional ceremonies that take place mainly during the dry season and during funerals.

- The Nguon festival in Foumban: This famous biennial cultural festival is a conference of the sovereign people before the Ku-mutngu. This festival has been in celebration since 1394 and has been perpetrated in the reign of all the monarchs who have succeeded Nchare Yen to this day.

- The Nyang-Nyang or Nekang or Nkee festival: It takes place every two years and means power. Performed by the Baleng or Bafoussam people, this initiatory ceremony dance coincides with the harvest period. Symbol of economic wealth, Nyang-Nyang is said to be the Raven's cry that helps women in the fields during harvest.

- The Ngou Nguong festival in Baleng: This biennial festival, which spans on several months, is aimed at introducing young people to the habits and customs of society.

- Kaing ceremony in Baham: Kaing means magic. It is a biennial rite of initiations, fertility cults and for the well-being of the people.

Agrotourism: Commonly referred to as Grassfields, given the predominance of agricultural plantations that extend over plains and valleys, agriculture is widespread in the Western Region. Its fertile land supports large-scale production of coffee, cocoa and tea, supplemented by food crops such as vegetables, cabbages, potatoes, peanuts, corn, beans and carrots.

Falls, waterfalls and lakes:

- The Mami Wata, Metche, Mouanko, Bakondji, Tchanko, Banka, Batoum, Pendou and Nde Falls.

- The Kigang and Batcha Waterfalls.

- The Dschang, Baleng, Doupe, Ghanka, Takouche, Nfou et Petpenoun Lakes.

Peaks, mountains and caves: The Neyang Peak, The Mete Mountains, Bamboutos, Kala and Mbapit, The cliff of Santchou, The rocks of Fongo Tongo, Ngang Batoufam, The caves of Banwa, Mboeto, and Ndessi Nekang.

Other sites: The Baleng and Bangou Chiefdom, The Bamileke huts from the Dschang market, Dschang Handicraft Center, Tea plantation of Djutitsa.

Adamaoua Region

The Adamaoua Region is a beautiful mountainous area, which marks the border between the forest of the south and the savannah of the north. It is called the Water Castle of Cameroon because it is where all the major rivers of the country take their source. It is also a hunting region for lovers of sport hunting.

County town: Ngaoundéré

Ngaoundéré, the railway terminal that connects the south to the north, is a pretty captivating city. It has a very lively Baladji neighborhood market, mosques, a museum and the Lamido Palace with its magnificent wall decoration illustrating the traditional architectural features of the region.

Falls and lakes

- Vina Falls: With a height of about 30 m, they offer a spectacular panoramic view.

- The Falls of Tello: Falls from a height of about 40 m, forming a cave with the rock in the shape of an arc.

- Lancrenon Falls: Falls from a height of around 50 m at the border with the Central African Republic.

24

- Koudini Falls: The water drops from a height of 40 m, into a huge rock table about 50 m in diameter.

- Lake Mballang: Beautiful crater lake in the middle of which is a small wooded island.

- Lake Tison: Small crater lake lined with trees and pleasant for relaxation.

Mountains, caves and rocks:

Majority of these mountains served as a refuge for the populations during the German colonial wars: Mont N'Gaoundéré, Mount Ngan-Ha, Mount Djoumbal, Mbe Cliff, Mayo-Djabo Cave, Raoumboum Cave or Mangbidoum, Damugare Cave.

The festivals :

- Nyem-Nyem Festival: Cultural event that commemorates the Nyem-Nyem people's victory over the colonizers, through the ascent of Mount Djim and a cultural exhibition (traditional dances, skits, fantasia, exhibition art).
- Mbor-Yanga Festival: Manifestations in Ngan-Ha during which the Belaka or Chief Superior Mboun enters into communion with his people to remember their glorious past.

South region

The southern part of the region is bordered by three countries: Equatorial Guinea, Gabon, and the Republic of Congo. The rainforest is the best area for agro and ecotourism. It offers visitors an appointment with the Pygmies, and numerous water courses that strengthen the climate and spectacular waterfalls.

County town : Ebolowa

Ecotourism: A dense forest area, the Southern Region offers visitors a magical setting for relaxation by the sea, with golden sandy beaches and forest walks.

- The Campo Ma'an Reserve: Forest reserve, with a rich animal biodiversity.

- The Dja reserve: Beautiful forest and animal heritage.

- Ebodje: Fishing village, with great beaches where sea turtles come to nest.

- The Lobe falls: Cliff of about 30 m, which flows into the ocean with incredible waterfalls. The Lobe river is unique in the world, as it flows directly into the sea.

- Pygmy camps: Discover and share the ancestral way of life of these forest people, through songs, traditional dances and expeditions in the forest.

Sports Tourism: Sport fishing is practiced in cities such as Kribi. Here, challenges are organized for amateurs in the Marina of Kribi. This gives place to the take of species such as tuna, marlin, barracuda, etc. Artisanal fishing is also practiced by the local population. Canoe races are included in festivals such as the Batanga Festival.

Seaside tourism: Kribi is the most important seaside town of Cameroon and one of the best in Equatorial Africa. This is mostly due to its beautiful sandy beaches along the ocean for miles.

Agrotourism: Ebolowa, Sangmelima, and Ambam are mainly farmers' and loggers' cities. They are ideal for exploring the wilderness.

Cultural tourism: This region is home to various rites and customs that can be experienced in the villages. It's also home to the markets of Abang Minlo and Kyeossi, which facilitate exchanges with Gabon and Equatorial Guinea.

Caves, Mountains and Peaks:

- The Nkolandom caves, 20 km from Ebolowa,

- Mount Ebolow'o, which overlooks the town of Ebolowa, gave it its name,

- The Ako'okas and Mazesse Rocks,

- The caves of Meyo Madjom, high of nearly 150 m and 2000 m of circumference,

- Njikom Bounou Mineral Water Source.

Falls: Memve'ele Falls (Consists of a series of spectacular falls, the largest of which has a magnetic field) and Nkoumouqui falls.

North-west region

This region is one of two English-speaking regions of the country. Located at an average elevation of 1550 m above sea level, the North-West is a highland region dominated by a mountain range.

Bamenda is an important road junction and commercial center. Ring Road is a road of 350km, that allows visitors to admire the region in all its diversity: Chiefdoms, landscapes, lakes, falls, reserves, etc.

County town : Bamenda

Tourist attractions :

- The Lakes: Lake Awing, Lake Oku, Lake Wum, Lake Bambalang, Lake Nyos

- The Falls: Menchum Falls, Abi Falls, Womenga Falls, Menchum Waterfalls

- The Reserves: Kilum Mountain Forest Project, Kimbi Game Reserve

- The Chiefdoms: Bali Chiefdom (It has a museum and an annual festival of traditional dances), Bafut Chiefdom, Mankon Chiefdom, Babungo Chiefdom, Laikom Chiefdom

- Other: Bamenda Fortress, Bamenda Handicraft Center and many more.

South-West Region

This region is one of two English-speaking regions of Cameroon. It's home to Limbe, the second largest beach resort in the country after Kribi. It is characterized by a rich vegetation cover and beautiful grey sand beaches bordering the Atlantic Ocean. This region has large green forests and various animal species. But most importantly, this region is home to Mount Cameroon, which is a volcano that is still active.

County town : Buea

Ecotourism:

- Mount Cameroon is the highest mountain in the country.

- The Korup National Park covers 1260 km². Its tropical rain forest is considered one of the most beautiful and oldest in the world. The richness of its fauna and flora lies in the fact that it survived the Ice Age and today, looks like a museum that is more than 60 million years old. Here, there are more than 400 species of trees and medicinal plants, more than 300 species of birds, 174 reptiles and amphibians and 114 species of fish.

- The Botanical Garden of Limbe was created in 1892 by horticulturists. This garden is particularly dedicated to the reproduction of plant species and is a must-see attraction.

- The Limbe Wildlife Centre is a center for animal collection and storage, that was built in 1993 to raise domesticated animals. Also, some of the animals were seized as part of the anti-poaching program, with the aim to then reintroduce them into the wild.

Agrotourism: This region is the country's ultimate agricultural industrial estate. The volcanic and fertile lands of the region have facilitated the establishment of several food companies for the production of tea, bananas, palm oil, as well as vast plantations of flowers, pineapples, palm trees, rubber trees, and many other fruits.

Seaside tourism:

- Limbe: It is known for its beautiful grey sand beaches from the various eruptions of Mount Cameroon. The city is shaded by large trees and is very popular. It is the second largest beach resort in the country after Kribi.

- Bakingili: Located about 30 km from Limbe, Bakingili Village is a small seaside resort to discover. Its proximity to the sea and the diversity of its flora are an ideal setting for relaxation.

- Idenau: Located at the border of Cameroon with Nigeria, Idenau is a regional port. Its beaches are constantly bordered by canoe carriers, local fishermen, and expatriates.

Cultural Tourism:

The cultural heritage of the southwestern region is strongly marked by the history of Colonialism in Cameroon.

- Bimbia: On the shores of the Atlantic, is the former slave station of Bimbia. Its forest preserved remnants of the slave trade, discovered in 1987. The site still bears indelible traces of the slave trade, through the buildings in which the slaves were parked before being shipped, as well as padlocks used to chain them and other slavers tools.

- Von Puttkamer's palace: Built in 1895 in Buea, this palace is a testimony of the German colonial era. Former residence of Governor Von Puttkamer.

- The German graves: The city of Buea was the political capital of Cameroon between 1901 and 1908. It is home to a German cemetery containing the graves of some Germans assigned to Cameroon.

Sports Tourism:

The ascension of Mount Cameroon, called the "Race of Hope," takes place every year in Buea. This international race is eagerly awaited in the country and ensures the visibility of the region.

Other Sites:

Mobombe waterfall, Nyarue waterfall, Ekumbe waterfall, Lake Barombi Kotto, Mundemba waterfall, Mana waterfall, Mets waterfall, Southern Bakundu forest reserve, Bomboko forest reserve, Takamanda forest reserve, The Inner salt lake, Ejagham lake, Miles six eight and eleven beaches, Twin lakes, John Holf beach, Suspension bridge, Okoyong caves, Mont Koupe.

Far North Region

This region's cultural diversity is exhibited through more than 50 ethnic groups, including the Kanuri, Fulani, Matakam, Kapsiki, Guiziga, and Moundang. With its hot and dry climate, the region is full of touristic wonders.

County-town: Maroua

Touristic sites:

- Waza National Park: Perfect for safari, Waza is one of Cameroon's most famous parks and the most spectacular in French-speaking Africa, with an area of 170000 hectares. You can discover wild species such as lions, elephants, hyenas, Buffon's kob, gazelles, giraffes, and many others.

- Rhumsiki is a lunar landscape consisting of peaks.

- Trekking: The most famous peak is the peak of Rhumsiki, 1224 meters above sea level.

- Hiking: It's practiced on the Mandara Mountains around Mora and the regions of Mogode, Mindif, and Kaele.

- The "Col of Koza" is a spectacular cliff, rich with its rugged terrain and traditional huts.

- The Oudjilla Kingdom has a polygamous leader with fifty wives and a hundred plus children.

- The Pouss village has Mousgoum huts with a traditional architectural style. These diverse landscapes are enriched by the artisanal production of blacksmiths, tanners, and potters of the region.

- The Kotoko Sultanates: In the Logone and Chari, the sultanates are full of treasures from the Sao civilization.

- The Lamidates: A visit to the Maroua, Mokolo and Yagoua lamidates will introduce you to the rich tradition of the Fulani people, Massa, Matakam, and others.

- The handicraft center of Djingliya.

CHAPTER 5: BUSINESS CHALLENGES

Cameroon is endowed with abundant natural resources, a steady economic growth, and a key location in Central Africa. However, the investment climate is plagued by corruption, heavy-handed bureaucracy, and poor infrastructure.

Infrastructure

Current infrastructure in Cameroon remains an important hindrance to growth. However, the 2009 Growth and Employment Strategy Paper revealed the extent of the government's public investment plan, aimed at securing the country's long-term growth through the development of infrastructure.

The Cameroonian government continues to invest heavily, as 2015 was notable for the number of completed projects. The year 2016 has seen further improvements to Cameroon's transport, telecoms, and energy networks.

Corruption

The lack of judicial capacity and poverty were some of the factors that made financial crimes, in the form of bribery, extortion, tax evasion and embezzlement, so rampant. Cameroon was ranked quite low by international organizations, as the country was overwhelmed with corruption.

However, although this is an ongoing fight, the government's anti-corruption laws are now being heavily reinforced through institutions such as The National Anti-corruption Commission (NACC).

Ease of Doing Business

Although there is still much room for improvement, efficient ways to simplify bureaucratic procedures have been put in place. For example, the CFCE (Center of Enterprise Creation Formalities), which is a one-stop shop that contains all the different administrations involved in the creation process of small and medium enterprises. Also, some tax exemption schemes have been put in place to encourage investments. Say more.

CHAPTER 6: STEP-BY-STEP BUSINESS REGISTRATION PROCESS

Over recent years, Cameroon has greatly improved its business creation process. However, it is important to understand the tax system, the different methods of company creation, and the registration process.

Theoretical creation

Before embarking on the registration process of your company, understanding some important requirements would be an advantage.

Legal requirements

1- The freedom of enterprise and its restrictions

- Respect for public order and good morals: The entrepreneur must be a model citizen and respect the laws in force in the country.

- Minors: Minors are not able to create businesses.

- Incompatibilities: Cameroonian police officers, magistrates, lawyers, soldiers at the front, and civil servants.

- Prohibitions: Prisoners cannot create businesses.

- Authorization to administer: A government authorization will be required for businesses such as pharmacies and banks.

2- Advantages and disadvantages of the different legal forms in Cameroon. The business law in force in Cameroon is the OHADA law (Organization for the Harmonization of Business Laws in Africa). It recognizes two categories of businesses: sole proprietorships (individuals) and corporations (legal entities).

- **Sole proprietorships or establishments:** These are companies with an annual turnover that is less or equal to 49 million CFA francs. In this category we find very small enterprises, small enterprises, and medium enterprises. An SPC in Cameroon is considered an "establishment." You are required to register your business in the Commercial Court Registry. You will need to provide your identification, birth certificate, marriage license, proof of address, criminal record, lease

32

documents, and the stamped application form you would have obtained at the Tribunal of Commerce Registry. This will cost about XAF 64,000.

ADVANTAGES	DISADVANTAGES
No minimum capital required	Unlimited liability of the entrepreneur. In case of bankruptcy, the assets of this one could be engaged.
Quick and simplified formalities	Access to credit or loans could be a bit more difficult
Low cost of incorporation	
Enticing and flexible tax system	

- **Commercial corporations or legal entities include**: Limited liability companies (LLC) and anonymous companies (AC).

    - LLCs include: single-member companies (held by a single individual or shareholder) and multi-personal limited liability companies (commercial companies created by several shareholders). To create a limited liability company (LLC), you will need a minimum capital of XAF 1 million. You must provide the company's name and initials, the company's legal status, details on the company's activities, the amount of the total capital invested, the head office address, business partners identity documents and personal details, and the company's executive members personal information and contact details. **(Decree N ° 2017/0877 / PM of February 28, 2017).**

ADVANTAGES	DISADVANTAGES
1 Million CFA francs minimum capital required	Cost of constitution quite high
Limited responsibilities	Partners can freely transfer their shares
The company may continue to exist, even in the event of an associate or manager's death or retraction. (unless the contrary is stipulated in the statutes)	
Transition to a notary for the statutes is optional	

    - Anonymous companies are associations of shareholders or owners with a specific status: they require a minimum capital of 10 million CFA francs (of which at least a quarter must be released during the creation), drafting of statutes by a notary and the opening of a business account in a commercial bank of the place.

ADVANTAGES	DISADVANTAGES
Great ability to mobilize funds	Minimum capital and cost of constitution high
Risk often limited to the contributions	Quite controversial in today's society, due to transparency issues, fraud etc.
Possibility to release only a quarter of the capital	Heavy system of administration for new businesses
	Double taxation

GOOD TO KNOW:

Tax headquarters depend on the business turnover:

- Small businesses: CDI Centre Divisionnaire des Impôts

- Medium-size businesses: CIME centre d'Impôts Moyennes Entreprises

- Major companies: DGE Direction de Grandes Entreprises

Control of the taxation system

Once you have determined the nature of your business and your sales turnover, you are to find out in which tax system your business fits:

- If your turnover is between 0 and 9,999,999FRCFA, your plan would be: income tax for small entities.

- If your turnover is between 10,000,000 and 50,000,000FRCFA, you are in a simplified tax regime.

- If your turnover is higher than 50,000,000FRCFA, you are under the direct tax scheme (régime reel). You can therefore engage in all types of public procurements.

Social Constraints

- Constraints related to labor inspections
- Constraints related to the CNPS (Cameroon's National Social Security Fund): Social Contribution registrations

Practical creation

Registration Process for Small and Medium-Sized Enterprises.

1-   Where should you go?

To register a business in Cameroon, it is simpler to contact the CFCE (Center of Enterprise Creation Formalities), which is a one-stop shop created in 2010, containing all the different administrations involved in the creation process of small and medium enterprises. Currently there are five centers located in the cities of Yaoundé, Douala, Garoua, Bamenda, and Bafoussam.

It should be noted that the members of the management committee of the CFCE are the Ministry of Small and Medium Enterprises of Social Economy and Crafts (MINPMEESA), the Ministry of Justice, the Ministry of Finance, the National Fund for Social Welfare and the Chamber of Notaries, which represents the private sector.

2-   What should you provide?

    a) Physical person

- Declaration of business creation – this can be done directly with the CFCE

- 2 original 4X4 identity photos

- Identity documents or passport/residence permit for foreign nationals

- Criminal record excerpt or Declaration of Honor –judicial history

- Original company's location plan

    b) Legal (moral) person

- Registration application

- Copies of the company's by-laws

- Declaration of regularity and conformity

- Criminal record of each partner and manager

- Photocopy of each associate's photo identity document

35

- Company's location plan

- 1 Post box

- 1 Telephone contact

3- How much will it cost?

a) Physical person: 42,000FRCFA

b) Moral or legal person: 55,000FRCFA

4- How long will it take?

Official duration: 72 hours (Could take 1 to 2 weeks)

Registration Process for Major investments or companies

1- Obtain a certificate of non-conviction to prove clean criminal record.

2- Procure valid entry and residential documents.

3- Reserve your company names by filing an application with the African Intellectual Property Organization (OAPI), at their headquarters in Yaoundé. This should take about six days.

4- Open a temporary business bank account. You will need a notary to draft a certificate that attests to the opening of a temporary bank account (account for the company in creation) with a local commercial bank. This document will certify that the company is in the process of creation. Deposit the business capital in this account and obtain a receipt. This usually takes a day.

5- An attorney or notary and all shareholders will be required to drafts the memorandum and articles of association, then sign the company bylaws before the notary. This should take about two days, and costs 2% of the capital if the amount is up to XAF 3,000,000, or 1.5% for capital from XAF 3,000,001 to XAF 10,000,000 + XAF 1000 per stamp for each page.

6- Submit an application for registration with the Trade and Personal Property Credit Register. This can be done at the Registry of the Court of First Instance in the area where the company will be established. You will then be issued a Certificate of Incorporation to publish in an official legal journal. This will take roughly one week.

7- File an application for an exoneration of the business tax for a period of two years. You will, however, still be required to declare your business activities on or before the 15th of every month. You will then obtain a taxpayer card. This will take roughly one week.

8- Present the physical location plan of your company to the tax department, and obtain an attestation of business premises. Under Cameroon law, it is important to have an address or a location for the business. Founders usually select the office of their notary or lawyer as the business location for incorporation purposes. The attestation is signed by an official of the tax district where the office is located. This will take approximately one day.

9- Have the signed bylaws duly registered with the Registration and Stamp Duty Office, at the Department of Taxation. Each page of the memorandum and articles of association must carry the current fiscal year's stamp. This will take approximately two days.

10- Declare the company's existence before the authorities in charge of your industry. Declare the company's existence to the local office of the Department of Labor. This will take approximately a day.

11- Register your employees with the health administration, then declare the existence of the company and the personnel before the National Social Insurance Fund (CNPS). This will take approximately two days.

12- You or your notary will file the registration documents to the One-Stop-Shop, also known as the CFCE (Centre de Formalités de Création des Entreprises). The CFCE will register the company with the RCCM (Trade Register and Property Credit), the Tax Administration, and the CNPS. This process will take approximately eight days, and will cost XAF 41,500.

13- Publish the incorporation of the company in one of the authorized newspapers, such as the Cameroun Tribune. This will take approximately three days, and cost XAF 57,000.

14- If you are into an import-export business, you will need a trade license, then you will have to get registered with the importers in order to obtain a SYDONIA number (i.e. custom computer identification). This is to facilitate the entry and exit of goods produced by the company in due and legal form. This process takes approximately 17 days.

Tax Registration and Trade Registration Requirements

1- Tax Registration

This will cost about XAF 1,500. You will be required to provide:

- A copy of your identification card
- Trade registration
- Site plan

2- Trade registration

This should be completed within 75 days. You will be required to provide:

- A certified copy of the company's statutes or founding act
- The company's regularity and conformity declaration

- A certified list of managers, directors, officers or partners, who have been declared personally responsible or have authority to bind the company or corporation for an indefinite period
- A sworn and signed statement certifying the company is not subject to any prohibition by law.

Investing in Cameroon

The role of the state is to create an enabling environment that allows businesses to flourish. This will then lead to the creation of jobs as investors, private entrepreneurs, and private companies are at the cornerstone of the economy's growth.

To invest in Cameroon as a foreigner, you will need to:

- Register with your embassy

- Contact the local business support organizations of your country, such as the American Chamber of Commerce in Cameroon

- Obtain an investment approval/declaration, before registering the company. Investors who intend to make direct investments of XFA 100 million or more must declare their intent to do so to the Ministry of Finance (MINFI) at least 31 days in advance. This process takes 31 days.

CHAPTER 7: LAWS AND REGULATORY BODIES

Laws and Regulations

Here are a few laws: Banking and credit laws, bankruptcy and collateral laws, commercial and company laws, labour laws, land and building laws, tax and trading laws.

Newspapers Legislation

In 2015, the government passed legislation expanding the number of newspapers that are allowed to publish the notice of incorporation of a business in Cameroon. In practice, most companies still choose to publish in the Cameroun Tribune.

OHADA

Article 10 of the Uniform Act of the OHADA (Organisation pour l'Harmonisation du Droit des Affaires en Afrique) states that "the articles of association shall be established by a notarial deed or by any other instrument that ensures the legal validity of the business where the registered office will be located. Such an instrument, together with a certification of the writing and signatures of all parties, should be deposited as originals in a notary's office. They may be amended only by the same procedure." From a legal perspective, commercial companies are governed by the OHADA Uniform Act.

Free economic zones

Such companies are eligible for many benefits such as exemption from permit requirements, the ability to open foreign currency bank accounts, and the right to transfer up to 75% of profits abroad.

Regulatory Bodies

CFCE: You or your notary must file registration documents to the One-Stop-Shop.

CNPS: Once you have hired your first employee, you will have to register them with the nearest CNPS (National Social Insurance Fund). You will also have to present your commercial registration certificate, your business permit, your taxpayer's card, your business location plan, and your lease documents if you are renting the office premises.

CHAPTER 8: TIPS AND ADVICE

The continent of Africa is an explosion of diversity, not only from one nation to another but also within each country. Cameroon is a perfect example of this diversity. Therefore, before going into business in Cameroon, it is important to be well prepared.

Checklist questionnaire:

- What type of business (and in what industry) are you hoping to invest?

- What is your target market audience?

- What size company?

- Will you be handling the business on site or from abroad?

- Will your business require employees?

- Will your business require a physical location/venue?

- Are you creating this business as a foreigner or as a citizen of the country?

- Are you familiar with the country?

- Is your business a new concept that will need to be introduced to the people?

- Will you be running the day-to-day activities of the business?

- Do you have help/contacts in your country of choice?

- Do you know how much capital will be required to start off?

- What is your capital?

Advise and recommendations:

In Cameroon, the best business ventures are often those that respond or bring a solution to an existing need. Having said that, the Cameroonian people are very open and appreciate original ideas, innovative ideas, new technology, and discovering new and different ways of doing things.

40

You can therefore be sure that your idea or business will be successful if you put in the work required:

- Understand who your target audience/market is.

- Locate the area of the country best suited to accommodate your business.

- Connect with people who could be of help.

- Choose the right publicity channels to make yourself and your business known.

- Also, going in with a partner can save you a lot of money and cut the workload considerably. Remember, you don't have to stay in a partnership forever, but it is an easier and quicker way to get started.

- When the country you're going into is foreign to you, it is important to know and understand the people you are going to be offering your services to, the culture, traditions, and ways of doing things.

- Do your homework: Anyone is free to set up a business in Cameroon, and foreigners are allowed to own 100% of a company's shares. The opportunities are endless. With this guide's information, you have a great starting point, but it is important to research in which of Cameroon's 10 regions you wish to target your business. Know the city and the people. The more you know, the better you will be able to target your efforts to the people most likely to buy your product or service.

- Choose your investment sector: The financial sector has different rules from the educational sector, for example, and this will impact the way you set up your business.

- Develop a detailed business plan: It must lay out your specific goals and be sure that they are realistic. While passion and ambition are essential, you must also have specific business objectives and a clear vision as to how to meet those goals.

- Communication: Communicating with everyone involved with the process of starting your business is crucial. You must use the same communication skills with customers as you do with investors. The best communication is the simplest. Keep it simple and keep it concise.

- Be competent and coherent when it comes to today's technology and processes: This is a vital step, even if your product is not in the high tech or digital field. Some of the means for marketing your

41

products or running your business will be digital, so you need to understand software and digital processes. You must be technologically literate, in order to compete in today's market. Customers will expect no less.

- Know your clients: Make it a point to know as much as possible about your clients and potential clients. Your customers are your business. Without them there is no business. Know and treat them well. Find the best means of communication with your customers.

- Know what you need: Entrants to the Cameroonian market might consider engaging locally hired representatives to provide guidance on the business environment, identify customers, and obtain market information. For products requiring after-sales service and spare parts, it is recommended that exporters consider operating through a distributor or dealership. Agents and distributors must register with the government and their contracts must be notarized and published in the local press.

Attention

Just as in any other country in the world, corruption does exist in Cameroon. It is advised you ensure that you go through the right channels and institutions whilst creating your business.

Should you decide to travel to Cameroon, be aware of all the visa requirements. Travelers should obtain the latest information on entry requirements from the nearest Cameroonian embassy or consulate.

If you are starting a business in Cameroon from abroad, ensure you use established companies or reliable contacts to help you register your business and or run your activities.

Finally

Setting up a business in Cameroon can be done relatively easily for any driven person. However, it is not an undertaking that can be taken lightly.

It takes time and patience to build a successful business in the Cameroonian market, but the advantage is that the market is wide open, diverse, and ready to receive new investors and entrepreneurs.

Constantly research market trends and best practices to improve your services and deliverables, then update your business plan to remain a step ahead of the competition.

Resources for Further Research

The organizations and resources listed below were used as reference for or have been partially introduced in this book. Should you need more information or require help to start your business in Cameroon or any other African country, please contact us via our website: www.startabusinessinafrica.com email: info@startabusinessinafrica.com or social media @SABIAFRICA1 and we will be more than happy to assist.

1) Cameroon Commonwealth (New Business Opportunities), *Cameroon Vision 2035*

2) *Cultures of the World: Cameroon*

3) Bradt guides: *Cameroon, Edition 3*

4) Africa Access

1.   CFCE: Centre de Formalités de Création d'Entreprises:
http://www.cfce.cm/formalites-en-ligne/

2.   African History. A Brief History of Cameroon.
http://africanhistory.about.com/od/cameroon/p/CameroonHist.htm

3.   Centurion Law Group. Cameroon Pushes for Infrastructure Progress.
http://www.centurionlawfirm.com/cameroon-infrastructure/

4.   Central Intelligence Agency. The World Factbook, Africa, Cameroon.
https://www.cia.gov/library/publications/the-world-factbook/geos/cm.html

5.   Country Meters. Cameroon population clock. http://countrymeters.info/en/Cameroon

6.   World Bank Group, Doing Business. Starting a Business in Cameroon.
http://www.doingbusiness.org/data/exploreeconomies/cameroon/starting-a-business/

7.   Expat.com. Setting up a business in Cameroon.
http://www.expat.com/en/guide/africa/cameroon/11741-setting-up-a-business-in-cameroon.html

8. **Food and Agriculture Organization of the United Nations. Cameroon.**
http://www.fao.org/countryprofiles/index/en/?iso3=CMR

9. **The FCBA Blog. http://www.fcpablog.com/**

10. **Global Timber. Cameroon. http://www.globaltimber.org.uk/cameroon.htm**

11. **British High Commission Yaoundé. Doing business in Cameroon.**
https://www.gov.uk/government/uploads/system/uploads/attachment_data/file/236804/FCO422_Doing_Business_in_Cameroon_web.pdf

12. **2016 Index of Economic Freedom. #130: Cameroon.**
http://www.heritage.org/index/country/cameroon

13. **The World Bank Group, Investing Across Borders. Cameroon.**
http://iab.worldbank.org/Data/ExploreEconomies/cameroon/starting-a-foreign-business

14. **International Democracy Watch. Central African Economic and Monetary Community.**
http://www.internationaldemocracywatch.org/index.php/central-african-economic-and-monetary-community

15. **Legal Zoom. Comparing an LLC to a Sole Proprietorship and a Partnership.**
https://www.legalzoom.com/knowledge/limited-liability-company/topic/llc-sole-proprietor-partnership-comparison

16. **MOJUFISC. Setting Up a Commercial Company in Cameroon and Privileges of Establishment.** http://mojufisc.com/en/setting-up-a-commercial-company-in-cameroon-and-privileges-of-establishment/

17. **Nations Encyclopedia. Cameroon – Environment.**
http://www.nationsencyclopedia.com/Africa/Cameroon-ENVIRONMENT.html

18. **One World Nations Online. Cameroon.**
http://www.nationsonline.org/oneworld/cameroon.htm

19. **Trading Economics. Cameroon GDP Annual Growth Rate.**
http://www.tradingeconomics.com/cameroon/gdp-growth-annual

20.   Transparency International. Cameroon: Overview of Corruption and Anti-Corruption.
http://www.transparency.org/whatwedo/answer/cameroon_overview_of_corruption_and_anti_corruption

21.   The Commonwealth. Cameroon: Constitution and politics.
http://thecommonwealth.org/our-member-countries/cameroon/constitution-politics

23.   Ventures Africa. A Look at Investment Opportunities in Cameroon.
http://venturesafrica.com/trade-investment-finance-cameroon/

24.   Ventures Africa. IMF Indicted in Cameroon's Fuel Subsidy Cuts.
http://venturesafrica.com/imf-indicted-in-cameroons-fuel-subsidy-cuts/

25.   World Population Review. Cameroon Population.
http://worldpopulationreview.com/countries/cameroon-population/

26.   Embassy of the United States, Yaoundé, Cameroon. Doing Business in Cameroon:
Exporting to Cameroon.
http://yaounde.usembassy.gov/doing-business-local.html

27.   http://www.lexology.com/library/detail.aspx?g=f1baf934-371d-42d3-827a-d06e95900c1e

28.   http://www.mintour.gov.cm/

29.   www.eiti.org/cameroon

www.ingramcontent.com/pod-product-compliance
Lightning Source LLC
Chambersburg PA
CBHW031500210526
45463CB00003B/1009